The Life of St. Faustina:

Messenger of Divine Mercy

By

Catherine Delacroix

Copyright © 2023
All rights reserved

Table of contents

Early Life and Vocation... 6
Life in the Convent.. 9
Spiritual Journey... 11
Mission of Divine Mercy..13
Persecutions and Suffering....................................... 15
Canonization and Legacy... 17
Divine Mercy Devotion... 18
The Diary of St. Faustina... 20
Visions and Mystical Experiences........................... 22
Trusting in God's Plan..24
St. Faustina's Relevance Today............................... 26
Conclusion... 28
Appendix.. 30

Early Life and Vocation

In this chapter, we explore the formative years of Helena Kowalska, who would later be known as Saint Faustina.

Helena was born on August 25, 1905, in Glogowiec, a small village in Poland. Her family, simple and devout, played a significant role in shaping her spiritual journey. Raised in a loving and religious environment, young Helena exhibited a deep sense of faith from an early age.

The call to religious life began as a whisper in her heart. Influenced by her family's piety and guided by her strong connection with God, she felt a growing desire to dedicate her life to serving the Church. This chapter explores the moments of clarity and conviction that led her to take the momentous step of leaving her home to join the Congregation of the Sisters of Our Lady of Mercy.

As we delve into her entry into the convent, we witness the challenges and adjustments Helena faced as she embraced a life of prayer, sacrifice, and service. Her initial days in the convent were marked by rigorous religious training and spiritual growth, setting the stage for her extraordinary journey of faith.

Within these walls of the convent, Helena began to experience a deeper connection with God. Her early encounters with divine grace and the call to a special mission are pivotal moments in her life. This chapter explores the first signs of her mystical experiences and the profound sense of purpose that would later lead to her becoming the apostle of Divine Mercy.

As Helena settled into convent life, the seeds of her vocation continued to grow. The novitiate period deepened her commitment to a life of poverty, chastity, and obedience, which are the core vows of her religious order. Guided by her superiors and mentors, she honed her spiritual discipline and embraced the daily routines of prayer, work, and communal living.

Helena's early years in the convent were characterized by her unwavering dedication and her genuine love for Christ. She was often found in the chapel, immersed in prayer and contemplation. Her deep devotion and spiritual sensitivity became increasingly evident to those around her.

Within the quiet walls of the convent, she began to receive mystical insights and graces, which would later be recorded in her famous diary. These experiences were both a source of solace and confusion for Helena. She struggled to comprehend the profound nature of her encounters with Jesus, who revealed to her His boundless Divine Mercy.

This chapter also explores the role of her spiritual mentors and confessors, who provided guidance and support during this formative period. It was under their wise counsel that Helena's understanding of her divine mission began to take shape.

The call to serve God in a unique and profound way was becoming clearer to Helena. Her early life and vocation were intertwined in a tapestry of faith, family, and the gradual unfolding of God's plan for her. In the subsequent chapters, we will delve deeper into her spiritual journey, the remarkable experiences she had, and how they paved the way for her to become a beacon of Divine Mercy to the world.

Join us on this captivating journey through the early life and vocation of Saint Faustina, a journey that lays the foundation for her remarkable mission and her enduring legacy in the Catholic Church.

Life in the Convent

In this chapter, we delve into Helena Kowalska's experiences as she embraced her new life within the Congregation of the Sisters of Our Lady of Mercy.

As Helena settled into convent life, the novitiate period marked the beginning of her formal religious training. During this time, she learned the rules and traditions of her religious order and deepened her understanding of the vows she had taken.

Her commitment to her religious vows of poverty, chastity, and obedience deepened as she embraced the daily routine of the convent. Life in the convent was not just about following rules and routines; it was also where Helena's profound encounters with Divine Mercy continued to unfold.

Her experiences within the convent walls became the crucible for her spiritual growth, and it was here that she began to document her spiritual journey in a diary, which would later become a central source of inspiration for the Divine Mercy devotion.

Within the quiet and contemplative atmosphere of the convent, Helena found solace in the routine of prayer, work, and community life. Her days began with the gentle tolling of the chapel bells, calling her to morning prayer. These moments of communion with God became the anchor of her daily existence.

As she interacted with her fellow sisters, she embraced the values of humility and service. Her willingness to perform even the most menial tasks with a spirit of love and devotion endeared her to her sisters and exemplified her commitment to the vows she had taken.

Life in the convent was not without its challenges, though. Helena faced the typical trials of communal living, including differences in personality and temperament. Yet, she met these challenges with grace and a heart full of forgiveness, always striving to live out the principles of Divine Mercy.

It was during her time in the convent that Helena's encounters with Divine Mercy continued to deepen. In moments of prayer and contemplation, she felt an overwhelming sense of God's boundless love and mercy. These experiences were transformative, strengthening her resolve to fulfill her divine mission.

The diary she diligently maintained during these years became a treasure trove of spiritual insights. In its pages, she recorded her conversations with Jesus and the profound revelations she received. These writings would later serve as a foundation for the Divine Mercy devotion, inspiring countless individuals to seek God's mercy and forgiveness.

In "Life in the Convent," we witness how St. Faustina's daily life, guided by her vows and immersed in prayer, prepared her for the extraordinary mission that lay ahead. This chapter provides a glimpse into the nurturing environment of the convent, where she cultivated her deep connection with God and set the stage for her role as an apostle of Divine Mercy.

In this chapter, we explore the challenges and spiritual growth that defined "Life in the Convent" for St. Faustina, setting the stage for her extraordinary mission of spreading the message of Divine Mercy to the world.

Spiritual Journey

St. Faustina's life was a remarkable odyssey of the spirit, a journey guided by divine encounters and a deepening connection with God Himself.

In the hallowed halls of her convent, she was no ordinary nun. Her spiritual journey was marked by extraordinary mystical experiences and visions that transcended the bounds of human understanding. It was within these ethereal moments that she communed with Jesus, the source of her boundless inspiration.

Mystical Experiences and Visions

In the stillness of prayer, St. Faustina received visions that unveiled the hidden mysteries of the divine. These transcendent encounters were not mere dreams but profound dialogues with Jesus Himself. In them, she glimpsed the radiant countenance of Divine Mercy and the profound depths of God's love. These experiences would serve as the foundation of her mission.

The Diary of St. Faustina

A sacred relic of her spiritual journey lies in the pages of her diary. It was within this simple book that St. Faustina recorded her innermost thoughts, her conversations with Jesus, and the revelations she received. This diary would later become a wellspring of inspiration for countless souls seeking solace and redemption in Divine Mercy.

Insights into Divine Mercy

As St. Faustina's spiritual journey unfolded, she became a vessel of divine wisdom. Her encounters with Jesus provided profound insights into the nature of Divine Mercy. Through her words, we come to understand the boundless love and forgiveness that God extends to all who seek Him. Her message of mercy would resonate far beyond the convent walls.

The Role of Spiritual Directors

Throughout her journey, St. Faustina sought guidance from spiritual directors and confessors. These wise mentors played a pivotal role in helping her navigate the complexities of her mystical experiences and divine calling. Their counsel provided her with the strength and clarity to fulfill her mission.

In the chapter of "Spiritual Journey," we bear witness to St. Faustina's intimate communion with the divine. Her mystical encounters, carefully chronicled in her diary, offer a glimpse into a profound and transformative spiritual odyssey. It is through her experiences that we come to understand the depth of her mission as an apostle of Divine Mercy, a mission that would touch the hearts of countless souls around the world.

Mission of Divine Mercy

St. Faustina's life was not confined to the quiet walls of her convent. It was a life ignited by a divine mission, a mission to proclaim and spread the message of Divine Mercy to a world yearning for redemption.

** *Spreading the Message* **

Guided by the revelations she received from Jesus, St. Faustina embarked on a mission to share the message of Divine Mercy with the world. She tirelessly conveyed the profound truth that God's mercy knows no bounds and that forgiveness is available to all who seek it.

** *Spiritual Direction from Fr. Sopoćko* **

St. Faustina found a trusted confidant and spiritual director in Father Michał Sopoćko, a priest who recognized the authenticity of her experiences. He played a crucial role in validating her mission and providing the guidance she needed to fulfill it.

** *Establishment of the Divine Mercy Devotion* **

At the heart of St. Faustina's mission was the establishment of the Divine Mercy Devotion. She worked tirelessly to convey the specific practices and prayers that would become integral to this devotion, including the Chaplet of Divine Mercy and the Feast of Divine Mercy.

Through her unwavering commitment, St. Faustina spread the message of Divine Mercy within her religious community and reached out to priests, theologians, and bishops to ensure its wider dissemination.

Impact and Challenges**

As St. Faustina's mission gained momentum, it encountered both fervent support and staunch opposition. She faced challenges within the Church and controversies that surrounded her. Despite these obstacles, her resolve remained unshaken, fueled by her unwavering faith in her divine calling.

In "Mission of Divine Mercy," we witness St. Faustina's transformative journey from a humble nun to a messenger of God's boundless mercy. Her mission transcended the confines of her time and place, leaving an indelible mark on the Catholic Church and the hearts of believers worldwide. This chapter illuminates the passion and determination with which she fulfilled her sacred task, forever changing the spiritual landscape for those who embrace the message of Divine Mercy.

Persecutions and Suffering

St. Faustina's path towards fulfilling her mission of spreading Divine Mercy was not without its trials and tribulations. In this chapter, we explore the challenges she faced and the profound suffering she endured in her unwavering commitment to her divine calling.

Opposition Within the Church

As St. Faustina sought to share the message of Divine Mercy, she encountered skepticism and opposition within the Church. Some questioned the authenticity of her mystical experiences, while others were hesitant to embrace the devotion she was promoting. We delve into the internal struggles she faced within the religious community.

** *Health Struggles**

Amidst her spiritual battles, St. Faustina also faced significant health challenges. Her fragile physical state added to the burdens she carried. Yet, she bore her ailments with grace and offered her suffering as a means of expiating the sins of others.

Trusting in God's Plan

Despite the trials and suffering, St. Faustina's trust in God remained unshaken. She saw her hardships as a reflection of Christ's own suffering on the cross, a way to unite herself with Him in the pursuit of souls' salvation. Her unwavering faith and perseverance in the face of adversity are a testament to her deep commitment to Divine Mercy.

In "Persecutions and Suffering," we witness St. Faustina's resilience in the face of challenges. Her journey was one marked by not only spiritual battles but also physical hardships. Her steadfast faith and trust in God's plan continued to shine as she carried the cross of suffering on her path towards fulfilling her mission. This chapter serves as a poignant reminder of the sacrifices she made for the sake of Divine Mercy and her unwavering dedication to her calling.

Canonization and Legacy

St. Faustina's life was marked by an extraordinary mission, and her legacy continues to inspire and transform lives to this day.

Beatification and Canonization

After her passing, St. Faustina's cause for beatification and canonization was set in motion. We explore the process of her beatification and eventual canonization, which were milestones that officially recognized her holiness and the authenticity of her mission.

The Impact of St. Faustina's Life

St. Faustina's life and message of Divine Mercy have left an indelible mark on the Catholic Church and the world. Her writings, especially her diary, have become spiritual classics and are widely read and cherished by believers seeking a deeper relationship with God.

The Divine Mercy Movement Today

St. Faustina's legacy lives on through the Divine Mercy devotion. We examine how this devotion has continued to grow and spread, touching the lives of millions of people who turn to Divine Mercy for solace, forgiveness, and hope.

In "Canonization and Legacy," we celebrate St. Faustina's official recognition as a saint and the enduring impact of her life and mission. Her canonization has solidified her place among the great saints of the Catholic Church, and her message of Divine Mercy continues to shine as a beacon of hope for a world in need of God's infinite love and forgiveness.

Divine Mercy Devotion

St. Faustina's life and mission were intrinsically linked to the establishment and promotion of the Divine Mercy Devotion, a profound spiritual movement that continues to touch the hearts and souls of believers worldwide.

The Heart of the Devotion

At the core of the Divine Mercy Devotion lies a simple yet powerful message: God's mercy is limitless and available to all who seek it. We explore how this central message, as revealed to St. Faustina through her mystical experiences, forms the foundation of the devotion.

* *The Chaplet of Divine Mercy***

One of the most iconic aspects of the Divine Mercy Devotion is the Chaplet of Divine Mercy. We delve into the history and significance of this prayer, which invites believers to meditate on the profound mercy of God and to intercede for the world.

The Feast of Divine Mercy

St. Faustina's mission included the establishment of the Feast of Divine Mercy, celebrated on the first Sunday after Easter. We examine the origins of this feast and how it serves as a special occasion for believers to receive abundant graces and mercy.

Embracing Divine Mercy Today

The Divine Mercy Devotion continues to grow and flourish in the modern era. We explore how individuals and communities worldwide have embraced this devotion, finding solace, healing, and spiritual renewal through their devotion to Divine Mercy.

In "Divine Mercy Devotion," we journey into the heart of St. Faustina's mission and her message of God's boundless mercy. This devotion, with its prayers and practices, has become a source of comfort and transformation for countless souls seeking to draw closer to the heart of God. It stands as a testament to St. Faustina's enduring legacy and her profound impact on the spiritual landscape of our time.

The Diary of St. Faustina

Within the pages of St. Faustina's diary lies a treasure trove of spiritual insights, mystical encounters, and a profound dialogue with the Divine. This chapter delves into the significance and impact of her diary on her life and the world.

In a quiet corner of the convent, amidst the rustling of pages and the flickering of a candle, St. Faustina meticulously recorded her thoughts, prayers, and conversations with Jesus. Her diary would become an intimate window into her soul and a profound revelation of Divine Mercy.

** *The Origins of the Diary* **

St. Faustina began her diary at the behest of her spiritual director, Father Michał Sopoćko. Its initial purpose was to record the details of her spiritual experiences, which were often too profound and transcendent to be contained in mere words.

** *Conversations with Jesus* **

The diary is a record of her intimate conversations with Jesus, where she sought guidance, solace, and a deeper understanding of His will. These dialogues revealed the depths of God's love, His desire for repentance and mercy, and His plan for her mission.

** *The Diary's Profound Insights* **

As we peruse the pages of her diary, we encounter profound spiritual insights and teachings that continue to resonate with believers. St. Faustina's writings explore themes of trust, humility, and surrender to God's will, offering timeless lessons for those seeking a closer relationship with Him.

The Diary's Impact

The diary has left an indelible mark on the spiritual landscape of the world. It has been translated into numerous languages and is widely read and cherished by believers seeking solace and inspiration. The diary's influence extends far beyond the convent walls, touching the hearts and souls of people from all walks of life.

In "The Diary of St. Faustina," we embark on a journey through the written testament of a humble nun who communed with the divine. It is a testament to the power of recording one's spiritual experiences and the profound impact that such writings can have on the world. St. Faustina's diary continues to serve as a beacon of hope, guiding believers on their own spiritual journeys towards God's boundless mercy.

Visions and Mystical Experiences

In the quiet corners of the convent, St. Faustina's life was illuminated by extraordinary visions and mystical experiences that transcended the realm of the ordinary. This chapter delves into the profound encounters she had with the divine.

** The Gift of Divine Insight**

St. Faustina's mystical journey began with the remarkable gift of divine insight. In moments of prayer and contemplation, she received visions that opened her eyes to the spiritual realities beyond the material world. These visions revealed to her the boundless depths of God's love and mercy.

** Encounters with Jesus**

At the heart of St. Faustina's mystical experiences were her encounters with Jesus Himself. In these extraordinary moments, she conversed with the Savior, who revealed Himself to her as the Merciful Jesus. Through these encounters, she gained profound insights into the nature of God's mercy and His desire for humanity's salvation.

** The Image of Divine Mercy**

One of the most iconic aspects of St. Faustina's mystical experiences was the request from Jesus to paint an image of Him as the Divine Mercy. We explore the significance of this image and how it has become a powerful symbol of God's love and forgiveness.

** The Revelations of Heaven, Hell, and Purgatory**

St. Faustina's mystical journey also included glimpses into the realities of heaven, hell, and purgatory. These revelations provided her with a profound understanding of the consequences of sin, the beauty of heaven, and the need for prayers and sacrifices for the souls in purgatory.

As we journey through "Visions and Mystical Experiences," we enter the realm of the extraordinary, where St. Faustina's encounters with the divine transcend the limits of human comprehension. Her mystical experiences are a testament to the profound depths of God's love and the boundless mercy that awaits those who seek Him. Through her visions, she became a messenger of hope and a conduit for the transformative power of Divine Mercy, a message that continues to inspire and console believers around the world.

Trusting in God's Plan

In the tapestry of St. Faustina's life, woven with mystical experiences and divine encounters, the thread of trust in God's plan stands out as a central theme. This chapter explores how her unshakable faith and trust became a guiding light through the darkest of times.

The Struggles of Trust

St. Faustina's journey was not without its moments of doubt and struggle. Despite her profound mystical experiences, she faced challenges and opposition within and outside the convent. We delve into the periods of uncertainty and the inner battles she waged on her path of trust.

The Message of Divine Mercy

At the heart of her mission was the message of Divine Mercy, a message that called on humanity to trust in God's boundless love and forgiveness. Through her mystical encounters, she learned that God's mercy knows no limits, and His plan for salvation extends to every soul.

Embracing Suffering and Sacrifice

St. Faustina's trust in God's plan was exemplified in her willingness to embrace suffering and sacrifice. Her fragile health and the trials she faced were seen not as obstacles but as opportunities to unite her suffering with that of Christ's for the salvation of souls.

Surrender to Divine Providence

As her journey unfolded, St. Faustina surrendered herself completely to Divine Providence. She trusted that God's plan, even in its mysterious and challenging moments, was for the greater good. Her unwavering trust became a source of inspiration for those around her.

In "Trusting in God's Plan," we witness St. Faustina's unwavering faith and her profound reliance on God's providence. Her life serves as a testament to the transformative power of trust, even in the face of adversity. Through her example, she invites us all to place our trust in God's plan, to embrace the crosses we bear, and to believe in the limitless mercy that awaits those who do.

St. Faustina's Relevance Today

As we draw near to the conclusion of St. Faustina's remarkable journey, we are left with a compelling question: What is her relevance to us in the present day? This final chapter explores how the life and mission of St. Faustina continue to resonate and inspire in our contemporary world.

*** The Enduring Message of Divine Mercy***

At the heart of St. Faustina's legacy is the timeless message of Divine Mercy. In an age marked by uncertainty, division, and spiritual longing, her message remains a source of hope and healing. We explore how her teachings on trust, repentance, and God's boundless love speak directly to the challenges and yearnings of our time.

A Saint for the Modern World

St. Faustina's canonization in the year 2000 by Pope John Paul II catapulted her into the consciousness of the modern Church. We examine how her life story, which unfolded in the early 20th century, has become a beacon of inspiration for the 21st century. Her relevance extends beyond the confines of time, culture, and geography, making her a saint for our contemporary world.

Embracing Mercy and Forgiveness

In a world marked by conflict and division, St. Faustina's emphasis on mercy and forgiveness is more crucial than ever. We explore how her teachings call us to embrace a spirit of reconciliation, compassion, and understanding in our personal lives and in society at large.

The Call to Holiness

St. Faustina's life was marked by her pursuit of holiness, a journey that is accessible to all. We reflect on how her example inspires us to embrace our own path of holiness, regardless of our circumstances or past mistakes.

In "St. Faustina's Relevance Today," we discover that her mission extends far beyond the borders of her time and place. Her life continues to touch hearts and transform lives in our modern world. Through her unwavering trust in God's plan and her message of Divine Mercy, she invites us to embark on our own journey of faith, hope, and love. St. Faustina remains a guiding star, illuminating the path toward a deeper relationship with God and a more merciful and compassionate world.

Conclusion

In the quiet town of Głogowiec, Poland, a humble girl named Helena Kowalska embarked on a journey that would transcend time and touch the hearts of countless souls around the world. Through the course of this book, we have traced the remarkable life of St. Faustina, a life marked by extraordinary encounters with the divine and an unwavering commitment to a mission of Divine Mercy.

From her early years in a loving but modest family to her entry into the Congregation of the Sisters of Our Lady of Mercy, St. Faustina's path was one of deep faith, sacrifice, and surrender to God's will. Her life was a testament to trust in God's plan, even in the face of suffering, opposition, and doubt.

As we explored the chapters of her life, from her mystical experiences and visions to her tireless efforts to spread the message of Divine Mercy, one theme became abundantly clear: St. Faustina was a messenger of hope. Through her, God revealed His boundless love and mercy, inviting all to draw near and seek His forgiveness and grace.

In our modern world, where chaos and confusion often reign, the life of St. Faustina serves as a guiding light. Her message of trust, her emphasis on mercy and forgiveness, and her call to holiness resonate deeply with the challenges and yearnings of our time. She is not a distant figure from the past, but a timeless beacon of inspiration for all.

St. Faustina's canonization in the year 2000 by Pope John Paul II elevated her to the status of a universal saint. She is a saint for the 21st century, a saint for the world. Her diary, filled with intimate conversations with Jesus, continues to touch lives, offering solace, guidance, and a profound understanding of God's plan for salvation.

As we conclude this journey through the life of St. Faustina, may we carry with us the lessons of her life: to trust in God's plan, to embrace Divine Mercy, to forgive and seek forgiveness, and to pursue holiness in our own lives. In doing so, we honor her legacy and, more importantly, respond to the call of Divine Mercy that beckons to each of us, inviting us to be vessels of God's love and compassion in the world.

St. Faustina's life was a testament to the transformative power of faith, trust, and Divine Mercy. May her story continue to inspire and guide us on our own spiritual journeys, drawing us closer to the boundless love of our Merciful Savior.

Appendix

In this appendix, we provide a curated list of resources for readers who wish to delve deeper into the life and teachings of St. Faustina and the Divine Mercy Devotion. These resources include books, websites, and organizations dedicated to preserving and promoting her legacy.

Books:

1. *Diary of Saint Maria Faustina Kowalska: Divine Mercy in My Soul* - St. Faustina's own diary, where she recorded her mystical experiences and dialogues with Jesus.

2. *St Faustina : Embracing Divine Mercy * by Samuel R. Devlin – A Novena containing prayers to St Faustina, From Day 1 to Day 9

3. *The Second Greatest Story Ever Told: Now Is the Time of Mercy* by Fr. Michael E. Gaitley, MIC - Explores St. Faustina's role in God's plan of Divine Mercy.

4. *Divine Mercy for Moms: Sharing the Lessons of St. Faustina* by Michele Faehnle and Emily Jaminet - A guide for mothers on embracing Divine Mercy in everyday life.

Websites:

1. [The Divine Mercy](https://www.thedivinemercy.org/) - The official website of the Marian Fathers of the Immaculate Conception, featuring information about St. Faustina, the Divine Mercy Devotion, and resources for prayer and reflection.

2. [The Diary of St. Faustina Online](https://www.faustina-message.com/the-diary/) - An online version of St. Faustina's diary for easy access and reading.

3. [EWTN Divine Mercy](https://www.ewtn.com/catholicism/devotions/divine-mercy-10067) - EWTN's resource page on Divine Mercy, including articles, prayers, and videos.

Organizations:

1. [The Congregation of the Sisters of Our Lady of Mercy](https://www.sisterfaustina.org/en/) - The religious order to which St. Faustina belonged, dedicated to promoting the Divine Mercy message.

2. [The Divine Mercy Apostolate](https://www.divinemercyapostolate.org/) - An organization committed to spreading the message of Divine Mercy through various initiatives and events.

3. [The Association of Marian Helpers](https://www.marian.org/) - The Marian Fathers' association dedicated to promoting Divine Mercy, offering spiritual resources, and supporting the cause of canonization of Blessed Michael Sopoćko.

These resources are intended to aid readers in their continued exploration of St. Faustina's life and her message of Divine Mercy. Whether you seek to deepen your understanding of her teachings, participate in Divine Mercy devotions, or engage with a community of like-minded individuals, these materials and organizations can provide valuable guidance and support.

If you need to contact me
Here is my email

alexk9adventures@gmail.com

Pls if you enjoyed this book kindly review it. Thank you

Catherine Delacroix

Made in the USA
Middletown, DE
10 January 2024

47637650R00020